49
DECLARATIONS
for
Courageous Christian Living

Scott Smylie
Send It Ahead Publications

Be strong and
couragous!

49 DECLARATIONS

for
Courageous Christian Living

Scott Smylie
Send It Ahead Publications

49 Declarations for Courageous Christian Living

First Edition, 2007

Library of Congress Cataloging-in-Publication Data
Smylie, Scott

49 Declarations for Courageous Christian Living
ISBN 978-0-9794263-0-8
1. Christian Life. 2. Success—Religious Aspects I. Title

Printed in the United States of America
Send It Ahead Publications

1 2 3 4 5 6 7 8 9 10

Acknowledgements

This book has been a labor of love, and many have helped bring it to pass. To Debbie Seaborn, Dana Prieto and David Distefano, thank you for your crucial guidance and technical skills that brought this from a simple manuscript to a substantive book. A heartfelt thank you goes to the many who read the early drafts and provided needed feedback, including Denise McCabe, Tom Eichem and Tammy Parlin.

To my parents, Ken and Marki Smylie, and my sister, Tiffany, thank you for your years of love and support. I could not be the person I am today without you.

To my favorite person, my lovely wife, Nichole, this book would never have been possible without your love and belief in me. Your words have inspired me to press on with God's calling.

To Jesus who has been the rock that has emboldened me to live the "courageous Christian life." I pray this book would bring glory to His name.

How to Achieve Maximum Value From This Book

Have you noticed how one bad thing, one negative comment—whether from a friend, loved one or mortal enemy—can counteract hundreds of good things in your life? That one negative thought plays over and over again in your mind.

Do you believe that your thoughts and words have power? Are you a victim of your thoughts and words? Many of us are still repeating the lie that "sticks and stones may break my bones, but words will never hurt me." Words have the power to wound, but they also have the power to change your life. Are you ready for a change? Are you ready to take your life to the next level?

If you are ready to change your life, then your words must change. However, before you can change your words, you must change your thoughts. After all, we usually speak whatever is on our mind.

There is a battle in our minds about whether we are going to think positive, life-giving thoughts or negative, life-destroying thoughts. The Bible tells us that out of the abundance of our heart (our thoughts), our mouth speaks (Matt. 12:34). It also tells us that life and death is in the power of the tongue. Are you choosing to think and then speak life?

Dr. Mark Virkler, a Christian researcher and author, notes that 80 percent of a Christian's thinking is negative. Can you identify with this in your own life? All these negative thoughts are tragic. If you receive Jesus as Lord and Savior in your life, your identity is transformed from someone distant from God because of your sin to a royal heir of God's kingdom. Your identity has been changed. When you think of yourself, do you think of yourself as a nobody or as a royal heir destined for greatness?

This change in identity requires a change in thinking. Do your thoughts reflect your new identity as a child of the King? The old, negative, sinful thinking (from when you were separated from God) will not move you toward the greatness and destiny God has planned for you. New, bigger and more powerful thinking is required. Your thinking should be consistent with who you *really* are now.

Just as thinking precedes action, identity precedes destiny. To help change your thinking and reveal your true identity to you, this book provides scripture-based declarations in three sections (Identity, Destiny and Provision) to replace the negative tapes playing in your head with the truth God has to say about you.

The **Identity** declarations provide true statements about who you *really* are as a new creation in Christ. These declarations are necessary to combat any lies you may believe about yourself.

Your destiny as God's child will manifest itself as your thoughts become actions. The **Destiny** declarations focus your mind on who you are becoming. To arrive at your destiny—your life's destination—you must start with the end in mind.

To achieve the dreams that God has placed in your heart, you will need the courage to chase after them and the boldness to ask God to provide the resources needed. Too often you *have not* because you *ask not*. The **Provision** declarations are designed to encourage you to think bigger and ask more often.

The **Provision** section is larger than the two previous sections because once you start down the path toward your dreams, obstacles often arise. More work may be required to strengthen your thought life during these challenges, so more mental ammunition is provided.

The power behind these declarations comes from aligning your life with God's plans for you. When you review the scriptures the declarations come from, you will notice many of them are conditioned upon obedience to God's direction. For example, in Matthew 6:33 you must *seek first* God's kingdom, *then* His provision will come. I encourage you to look up the scriptures surrounding the ones cited here to see their context. After all, the Bible teaches us that we are part of God's master plan, and when we are in agreement with God's plan for us, the impossible becomes possible. Our lives then achieve their highest potential and are spent on eternally significant endeavors.

As you meditate on the 49 declarations in this book, simply choose one or two to focus on each week. Read them out loud in the morning before your day begins and again at the end of the day. In fact, I dare you to choose the two most meaningful declarations to you in this book and read them out loud twice a day for 21 days.

To let me know how these declarations changed your life, please e-mail me at **comments@courageouschristianliving.com**.

For as he thinks within himself, so he is.

—Proverbs 23:7 (NASB)

We sow our thoughts, and we reap our actions;
We sow our actions, and we reap our habits;
We sow our habits, and we reap our characters;
We sow our characters, and we reap our destiny.

—Charles Albert Hall

In the Messiah, in Christ, God leads us from place to place in one perpetual victory parade. Through us, he brings knowledge of Christ.

&

2 Corinthians 2:14 (The Message)

Identity

I am a winner.

I am victorious.

God makes me a champion.

1

Even as [in His love] He chose us [actually picked us out for Himself as His own] in Christ before the foundation of the world, that we should be holy (consecrated and set apart for Him) and blameless in His sight, even above reproach, before Him in love.

Ephesians 1:4 (AMP)

Identity

I was chosen to be
one of God's happy thoughts
before the universe was created.

2

Paul addresses his letter to:

…The saints in Ephesus, the faithful in Christ Jesus.

Ephesians 1:1 (NIV)

Paul addresses his letter to:

…All the saints in Christ Jesus at Philippi, together with the overseers and deacons.

Philippians 1:1 (NIV)

Identity

I am a saint, a holy child
of the Almighty Father,
and I am choosing
to align my actions
with who I truly am.

3

...To all of you that are in Christ Jesus (the Messiah), may there be peace (every kind of peace and blessing, especially peace with God, and freedom from fears, agitating passions, and moral conflicts). Amen (so be it).

1 Peter 5:14 (AMP)

Identity

I am enjoying Jesus' peace,

love and approval,

which pushes out all fears,

concerns and irritants of daily life.

4

I no longer call you servants, because a servant does not know his master's business. Instead, I have called you friends, for everything that I learned from my Father I have made known to you.

John 15:15 (NIV)

Identity

I am Jesus' friend,
and I receive the God-size dreams
He has for me.

5

Do you not know that your body is the temple (the very sanctuary) of the Holy Spirit Who lives within you, Whom you have received [as a Gift] from God? You are not your own.

1 Corinthians 6:19 (AMP)
(Also see Romans 8:9, 11)

Identity

I am the temple of God;

therefore I love, value

and maintain my body.

6

Then Jesus turned to the Jews who had claimed to believe in him. "If you stick with this, living out what I tell you, you are my disciples for sure. Then you will experience for yourselves the truth, and the truth will free you."

John 8:31-32 (The Message)

Identity

When I experience the Truth
about myself, I am set free
to achieve my ultimate potential.

7

For we are God's [own] handiwork (His workmanship), recreated in Christ Jesus, [born anew] that we may do those good works which God predestined (planned beforehand) for us [taking paths which He prepared ahead of time], that we should walk in them [living the good life which He prearranged and made ready for us to live].

Ephesians 2:10 (AMP)

Identity

God has placed dreams
in my heart, and He is faithful
to bring them to completion.

8

Now if we are children, then we are heirs—heirs of God and co-heirs with Christ, if indeed we share in his sufferings in order that we may also share in his glory.

Romans 8:17 (NIV)

Identity

Today I choose to receive my inheritance as a royal child and a joint heir with Jesus of God's kingdom and birthright.

I choose to accept the rights, honors and provisions of royalty appropriate to my position, and I banish all thoughts of myself as lacking, wanting or being incomplete.

9

The wicked borrow and do not repay,

but the righteous give generously.

❧

Psalm 37:21 (NIV)

Identity

I am a vessel of goodness,
giving value to everyone around me.

10

Christ has set us free to live a free life. So take your stand! Never again let anyone put a harness of slavery on you.

Galatians 5:1 (The Message)

Identity

Right now I am enjoying the freedom
to be who God really created me to be.
I am free from sin and the lies
I used to believe, and my destiny
is calling me to action.

11

No one who is born of God will continue to sin, because God's seed remains in him; he cannot go on sinning, because he has been born of God.

1 John 3:9 (NIV)

Identity

Sin, defeat and failure are immediately leaving my life because they are not consistent with my new identity in Christ.

For God so loved the world that he gave his one and only Son, that whoever believes in him shall not perish but have eternal life.

∂∽∻

John 3:16 (NIV)

Identity

I am deeply loved and valued by God.

13

I'm absolutely convinced that nothing—nothing living or dead, angelic or demonic, today or tomorrow, high or low, thinkable or unthinkable—absolutely nothing can get between us and God's love because of the way that Jesus our Master has embraced us.

Romans 8:38 (The Message)

Destiny

This day I boldly and courageously walk through life knowing that nothing can separate me from God's love, approval and acceptance.

14

Now faith is the assurance (the confirmation, the title deed) of the things [we] hope for, being the proof of things [we] do not see and the conviction of their reality [faith perceiving as real fact what is not revealed to the senses].

Hebrews 11:1 (AMP)

Destiny

I am looking with my eyes of faith, and I see a bright future ahead of me.

15

For whatever is born of God overcomes the world; and this is the victory that has overcome the world—our faith.

1 John 5:4 (NASB)
(Also see Romans 8:37 and 2 Corinthians 2:14)

Destiny

I choose to overcome the obstacles in my life and walk out my personal victory through my faith in Jesus Christ.

16

For as he thinks within himself, so he is.

∂∽∾

Proverbs 23:7 (NASB)

Destiny

Today I choose to focus my thoughts on my dreams, knowing that my actions will follow my thoughts.

17

45

I can do all things through Him who strengthens me.

෧෧

Philippians 4:13 (NASB)

Destiny

I am fearlessly fulfilling God's plan
and destiny for me because
He gives me the strength and ability
to go beyond my own limitations
and accomplish great things.

18

Therefore if any person is [ingrafted] in Christ (the Messiah) he is a new creation (a new creature altogether); the old [previous moral and spiritual condition] has passed away. Behold, the fresh and new has come!

2 Corinthians 5:17 (AMP)

Destiny

Right now I choose Jesus
and the life He offers me,
leaving behind the past and all its
burdens. As a completely loved person, I
am free to achieve my full potential.

19

Jabez cried out to the God of Israel, "Oh, that you would bless me and enlarge my territory! Let your hand be with me, and keep me from harm so that I will be free from pain." And God granted his request.

1 Chronicles 4:10 (NIV)

Destiny

Lord, bless me and increase my wealth. Guide me from trouble and protect me from pain.

20

Finally, brothers, whatever is true, whatever is noble, whatever is right, whatever is pure, whatever is lovely, whatever is admirable—if anything is excellent or praiseworthy—think about such things.

Philippians 4:8 (NIV)

Destiny

In this very moment I choose to think and speak only words of purity, harmony, beauty and excellence.

21

Therefore, there is now no condemnation

for those who are in Christ Jesus,

because through Christ Jesus

the law of the Spirit of life set me free

from the law of sin and death.

Romans 8:1-2 (NIV)

Destiny

I am freely enjoying a life
of peace and love,
and I reject any condemning
or critical thoughts
because they are not of God.

22

No weapon forged against you will prevail, and you will refute every tongue that accuses you ....

Isaiah 54:17 (NIV)

No, in all these things we are more than conquerors through him who loved us.

Roman 8:37 (NIV)

Destiny

No plan or conspiracy
against me will succeed,
for I am more than a conqueror!

23

With long life will I satisfy him
and show him my salvation.

Psalm 91:16 (NIV)

Nevertheless, I will bring health and healing
to it; I will heal my people and will let them
enjoy abundant peace and security.

Jeremiah 33:6 (NIV)

Destiny

I am enjoying a long and abundant life with great health and healing power flowing through me.

24

Whatever you do, work at it with all your heart, as working for the Lord, not for men, since you know that you will receive an inheritance from the Lord as a reward. It is the Lord Christ you are serving.

&

Colossians 3:23-24 (NIV)

Destiny

Today I choose to diligently work for God, knowing that God sees my efforts. No matter what else happens, He loves me, approves of me and will reward me.

25

And God raised us up with Christ
and seated us with him in the heavenly
realms in Christ Jesus.

Ephesians 2:6 (NIV)

Destiny

My eternal destiny is secure
with Jesus in heaven,
so I can boldly follow
the dreams He gives me.

26

The tongue has the power of life and death, and those who love it will eat its fruit.

Proverbs 18:21 (NIV)

Destiny

I am speaking my dreams
of life and victory out loud.
I can taste my destiny.

27

You gave them bread from heaven for their hunger and brought water for them out of the rock for their thirst; and You told them to go in and possess the land You had sworn to give them.

Nehemiah 9:15 (AMP)

Provision

I declare the Lord will take care of me today in His own miraculous way. He is bringing me my destiny.

28

Instead of your [former] shame
you shall have a twofold recompense;
instead of dishonor and reproach
[your people] shall rejoice
in their portion. Therefore in their land
they shall possess double [what they had
forfeited]; everlasting joy shall be theirs.

Isaiah 61:7 (AMP)

Provision

God is replacing my shame and poverty

with a double portion

of joy and abundance.

29

Be cheerful no matter what; pray all the time; thank God no matter what happens. This is the way God wants you who belong to Christ Jesus to live.

❧

1 Thessalonians 5:16-18 (The Message)

Provision

I am thankful for all the good in my life. My prayers of thanksgiving release me from bitterness, rage and hostility, and bring peace, joy and God's abundant provision.

30

71

The **LORD** is my shepherd,

I shall not be in want.

He makes me lie down in green pastures,

he leads me beside quiet waters,

he restores my soul.

He guides me in paths of righteousness

for his name's sake.

Psalm 23:1-3 (NIV)

Provision

The Lord is restoring my soul;
I am enjoying rest and peace beside His
green pastures and still waters.
His provision, grace and love make me
whole, full and complete.

31

GOD met me more than halfway,

he freed me from my anxious fears.

Look at him; give him your warmest

smile. Never hide your feelings from him.

When I was desperate, I called out, and

GOD got me out of a tight spot.

Psalm 34:4-6 (The Message)

Provision

I look to the Lord
when I am troubled or suffering,
knowing that God hears my prayers
and saves me from my fears.

32

Delight yourself also in the Lord, and He will give you the desires and secret petitions of your heart.

Psalm 37:4 (AMP)

Provision

I am enjoying my time with God
and trust him to bring me
my deepest desires.

33

Be still before the LORD and wait patiently for him; do not fret when men succeed in their ways, when they carry out their wicked schemes.

Psalm 37:7 (NIV)

Provision

My faith is increasing

as I cease striving

and I receive the Lord's provision.

34

In the multitude of my
[anxious] thoughts within me,
Your comforts cheer
and delight my soul!

——

Psalm 94:19 (AMP)

Provision

When fear, worry and anxiety

enter my mind,

I choose to focus on God's

comfort, love and acceptance

and receive peace, joy and security

in my innermost being.

35

The lions may grow weak and hungry,

but those who seek the LORD

lack no good thing.

ఆఈ

Psalm 34:10 (NIV)

Provision

While the fierce and powerful
around me may fail,
I know that God will fill my life
with good things.

36

And my God will liberally supply (fill to the full) your every need according to His riches in glory in Christ Jesus.

❧

Philippians 4:19 (AMP)

Provision

Today I am enjoying and receiving
God's abundant love and provision,
which meets and exceeds all my needs.

37

No test or temptation that comes your way is beyond the course of what others have had to face. All you need to remember is that God will never let you down; he'll never let you be pushed past your limit; he'll always be there to help you come through it.

1 Corinthians 10:13 (The Message)

Provision

I can overcome any challenge
because God knows my limits,
and He will make a way
for me to survive and thrive.

38

You will be blessed in the city
and blessed in the country.

Deuteronomy 28:3 (NIV)

The LORD will command the blessing
upon you in your barns and in all that you
put your hand to, and He will bless you in the
land which the LORD your God gives you.

Deuteronomy 28:8 (NASB)

Provision

Everywhere I go,
blessings and abundance find me
and fill my life with goodness and love.

39

I will repay you for the years the locusts have eaten....

Joel 2:25 (NIV)

Provision

God is restoring and repairing
what is missing in my life.

40

…The prayer of a righteous man
is powerful and effective.

James 5:16 (NIV)

Provision

I pray boldly to God,
believing that He hears my requests
and that powerful, life-changing,
mountain-moving results are occurring.

41

And He said to them, "Because of the littleness of your faith; for truly I say to you, if you have faith the size of a mustard seed, you will say to this mountain, 'Move from here to there,' and it will move; and nothing will be impossible to you."

Matthew 17:20 (NASB)

Provision

I am visualizing my dreams,

and I have faith

they will come to pass.

42

Ask and it will be given to you;

seek and you will find;

knock and the door will be opened to you.

For everyone who asks receives;

he who seeks finds;

and to him who knocks,

the door will be opened.

Matthew 7:7-8 (NIV)
(Also see Luke 11:9-10)

Provision

I boldly *ask* God

to take care of my needs and desires.

I am *looking* for His answers,

and I courageously *take action,*

knowing that God wants to bless me.

43

But seek (aim at and strive after)

first of all His kingdom

and His righteousness

(His way of doing and being right),

and then all these things taken together

will be given you besides.

Matthew 6:33 (AMP)

Provision

Today I am following God, knowing He will take care of all my needs.

44

But remember the **LORD** your God, for it is he who gives you the ability to produce wealth, and so confirms his covenant, which he swore to your forefathers, as it is today.

Deuteronomy 8:18 (NIV)

Provision

I am grateful
for all God's provisions,
and I acknowledge my wealth
comes from Him.

45

God is a safe place to hide,
ready to help when we need him.
We stand fearless at the cliff-edge of
doom, courageous in seastorm and
earthquake, Before the rush and roar of
oceans, the tremors that shift mountains.
Jacob-wrestling God fights for us,
GOD of angel armies protects us.

Psalm 46:1-3 (The Message)

Provision

When things get tough and the world
is crashing down around me,
I am courageous because God is my
refuge, my strength and my protector.

46

Do not withhold good
from those who deserve it,
when it is in your power to act.

Proverbs 3:27 (NIV)

Provision

Right now I choose to give

all the good I can,

to as many people as I can,

as quickly as I can.

47

And without faith
it is impossible to please Him,
for he who comes to God
must believe that He is
and that He is a rewarder
of those who seek Him.

Hebrews 11:6 (NASB)

Provision

I believe God will reward me for seeking Him.

48

Do not be seized with alarm and struck

with fear, little flock,

for it is your Father's good pleasure

to give you the kingdom!

ଚ୬ଙ

Luke 12:32 (AMP)

Provision

I am bold and courageous because my
God has given me His kingdom,
and no matter what happens
I will always have a home with Him.

49

My Scripture for Courageous Christian Living

Write down your favorite encouraging scripture.

_____

_____

_____

_____

_____

_____

_____

_____

My Declaration for Courageous Christian Living

Write down a declaration or statement of faith about you taking action on that verse.

_____

_____

_____

_____

_____

_____

_____

_____

_____

My Scripture for Courageous Christian Living

Write down your favorite encouraging scripture.

_____

_____

_____

_____

_____

_____

_____

_____

_____

My Declaration for Courageous Christian Living

Write down a declaration or statement of faith about you taking action on that verse.

_____

_____

_____

_____

_____

_____

_____

_____

My Scripture for Courageous Christian Living

Write down your favorite encouraging scripture.

_____

_____

_____

_____

_____

_____

_____

_____

My Declaration for Courageous Christian Living

Write down a declaration or statement of faith about you taking action on that verse.

_____

_____

_____

_____

_____

_____

_____

_____

_____

My Scripture for Courageous Christian Living

Write down your favorite encouraging scripture.

_____

_____

_____

_____

_____

_____

_____

_____

My Declaration for Courageous Christian Living

Write down a declaration or statement of faith about you taking action on that verse.

_____

_____

_____

_____

_____

_____

_____

_____

_____

_____

Questions for Thought

Which declaration was the most meaningful to you? Why?

_____

_____

_____

_____

_____

Do some of the declarations seem too good to be true? If so,
which ones? _____

_____

_____

_____

_____

Questions for Thought

Do you hold any beliefs about God or yourself that may not be accurate? _____

_____

_____

_____

_____

Now that you have read this book, have any beliefs about God or yourself changed? If so, describe. _____

_____

_____

_____

_____

Questions for Thought

What is the percentage of your thoughts that are positive, God-centered thoughts versus negative self-centered thoughts? Why? _____

_____

_____

What steps can you take to align your thoughts with what God says is true about you? _____

_____

_____

_____

_____

_____

_____

Questions for Thought

Imagine a bold, courageous Christian life. What needs to change in your life for this to occur? _____

_____

_____

_____

_____

What is *one* thing that you will change in your life this week as a result of reading this book? _____

_____

_____

_____

_____

ADDITIONAL RESOURCES:

For free tips, tools and to order additional books, audio products, small group study guides or for more information about Courageous Christian Living, please check out **www.courageouschristianliving.com.**

BOOKING INFORMATION:

To have Scott Smylie come to your church or company for seminars, workshops, breakout sessions or keynote speeches, click on the "speaking" link at **www.courageouschristianliving.com.**

COURAGEOUS

CHRISTIAN LIVING

JOSHUA 1:7